JANET AUTHERINE

GROWING INTO GREATNESS WITH GOD

7 Paths to Greatness for Our Sons & Daughters

Growing into Greatness with God—
Seven Paths to Greatness for Our Sons and Daughters
2nd Edition
Text copyright @ 2018 by Janet Autherine

Visit us on the web:
www.GrowIntoGreatness.com
www.JanetAutherine.com

Unless otherwise noted, scripture quotations and Bible stories
are taken from the King James Version of the Holy Bible.
Some artwork is from www.Shutterstock.com

ISBN: 13: 978-0-9912000-4-7
LCCN: 2018904673
Autherine Publishing LLC, Winter Springs, FL

Printed in the United States of America
October 2018

Second edition

Growing Into Greatness with God

Janet Autherine

Autherine
PUBLISHING

Seven Paths to Greatness
for Our Sons and Daughters

DEDICATED TO GABRIEL, GIORGIO, AND GIAN

You are "Boys Rising!"— rising to be the young men of strong character that God wants you to be. Your smiles bring sunshine into every dark place; use them abundantly. You are perfectly made. You are loved beyond imagination. As you grow do not forget the joy of solving a puzzle: if you call on God and it seems that he is silent it is because he has already provided you with the answer. You just have to construct the pieces of the puzzle. Stand tall knowing that you are a child after God's own heart and have already been given everything that you need to succeed. Don't be afraid to grow into your greatness.

Love, Mom

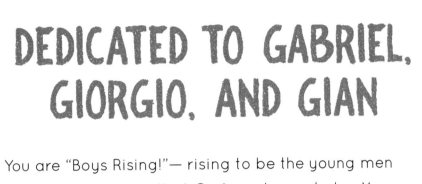

A GIFT FOR

_____

FROM

_____

DATE

_____

CONTENTS

SONS AND DAUGHTERS,

YOU ARE A CHILD AFTER GOD'S OWN HEART, AND YOU CAN BE ALL THAT GOD WANTS YOU TO BE!

You are not alone in this world; you are the vine from a tree that connects all mankind. Long before you were born, God wrote greatness next to your name. You are a unique being, and there is a special light in your soul that can light your path and radiate through everyone that comes into your presence. No one can define you but you; therefore, you are the only one who can determine what greatness means to you. Your challenge is to identify and embrace your unique talents and find the path to your own personal greatness.

As a child, I loved reading bible stories because they inspired and motivated me and allowed me to dream big dreams. I loved reading about ordinary people doing extraordinary things. In this book, I have shared my favorite stories in the hopes that they will also inspire you.

Enjoy the journey of discovering all the wonderful complexities of your being. As you continue to grow in grace, you will discover that the love in your heart is boundless, and your strength can quietly move mountains. Give your mind permission to travel where the body cannot go and be open to all the wisdom that the universe has to offer. God values the contents of your heart so fill it with love. I hope that you will carry these words in your heart, be inspired to be your best self, and grow into greatness with God.

GROWING IN LOVE

THE JOURNEY BEGINS

Do you like superheroes? Let us take a journey together and discover some unlikely super heroes of the Bible. At the end of our journey, I want you to understand the value of being kind, loving, and courageous. I want you to stand tall, walk with a spirit of gratitude and grow more confident in your ability to be a leader.

~~~~~~~~~

Let love and faithfulness never leave
you; bind them around your neck,
write them on the tablet of your heart.
Then you will win favor and a good
name in the sight of God and man.

Proverbs 3: 3-4

~~~~~~~~~

OUR HERO

SAMUEL was a man of God. One day, God sent Samuel to anoint a king. Samuel started his search at the house of Jesse. Jesse had seven sons that he thought had a "kingly" appearance, but when he took them to Samuel, God told Samuel that they were not the chosen ones. Reluctantly, Jesse took David to Samuel. David was a shepherd and a small boy. However, God looked beyond David's outward appearance and focused on the boy's heart. In David's heart, God saw a boy who was strong, courageous, and loyal and who loved God above everything else. God saw that David was growing into greatness.

OUR LESSON

You Have a Beautiful Heart

What is in your heart? Is it filled with love for everyone, even those who do not look or act like you? Would others describe you as someone who loves God above everything else? Do you have dreams of being a doctor, a firefighter, an astronaut, or even the president of a country? Dream on! When you can, add to your dreams concrete steps to achieve your goals. There are people who will try to define you by your outward appearance and your worldly possessions, but only you and God know the contents of your heart. And it is those contents that will lead you to greatness.

OUR HERO

JESUS was born to parents Mary and Joseph. He was a love offering from God to all of us. Jesus spent his life sharing his love with everyone, especially the sick, the poor, and those who were considered outcasts in society. There are numerous other stories of Jesus healing the sick, feeding the hungry, and offering hope to the hopeless. Jesus left us with a great commandment: **"Love the Lord God with all your heart and love your neighbor as yourself."**

MATTHEW **22:36-40**

OUR LESSON

You Are Love in Action

We don't always get to choose our neighbors, so loving your neighbor could mean smiling at someone who never returns the smile, cheering for the team that just beat you in a hard fought game, sitting next to the child who is always alone, or showing kindness to the local bully. However, loving your neighbor is also giving the gift of love to yourself. We spring from one great tree of life; when the root of the tree is watered with love, we all thrive.

Remember that love is a reflection of your actions, not just your words. Loving God and your neighbor is the answer to most of the meaningful questions in life and the solution to many of the world's problems. Whether you are trying to bring peace to the world or to your own family, the solution is rooted in love.

THREE WAYS TO GROW IN LOVE

1. Step outside of your inner circle: Perform an act of kindness for a stranger. Sit or play with someone new at lunchtime. Tell someone something that you like about them.

2. Write three things that you love about yourself; it will make you smile when you are feeling insecure.

3. Become pen pals with someone in another country to expand your community and world-view.

MY NOTES

GROWING IN FAITH

Therefore I tell you, whatever you ask for
in prayer, believe that you have received it,
and it will be yours.

Mark 11:24

OUR HERO

God told **NOAH** that a great flood was coming and asked him to build an
ark. Upon building the ark, he was to fill it with two of every species of
life. Noah walked in faith and built a large ark as God commanded, even
though there were no visible signs of a storm. It took many years to build
the ark, and Noah was constantly teased and ridiculed by most people
in his community. Noah did not let the negative people win; he held on to
his faith and continued his work. Eventually, a storm came and it rained
continuously for 40 days and 40 nights and the entire land was flooded.
Unfortunately, only Noah, his family, and the species in the ark survived.
After the flood, a beautiful rainbow appeared in the sky and God promised
that he will never again destroy the entire earth by flood.

GENESIS 6-8

Walk in Faith

Our world expands beyond what we can see or imagine. Since only a small part of the universe can be viewed with the naked eye, you have to be willing to walk in faith. Sprinkled in with the beauty and joy of life will be storms that will require you to anchor yourself in your faith until your rainbow arrives. Sometimes, God speaks to us and offers a solution through unexpected people and unusual circumstances. When your Noah moment arrives, keep your mind and heart open to experience all that the universe has to offer, both the seen and unseen.

OUR HEROES

ABRAHAM and his wife, **SARAH**, had a great life in the city of Ur, but their greatest desire was to have a son. God asked Abraham to take his wife and move to an unknown land where they would soon have a son, and eventually his family members would be as numerous as the stars in the sky. Abraham had doubts, but he trusted in God. It was a long journey. Famine ravished the land, and Abraham made some mistakes along the way. Abraham became impatient and doubted that God would keep his promise of providing him with a son. Abraham also lied when he told some men, who made him fearful, that his wife Sarah was his sister. God forgave Abraham for his mistakes. Abraham's trust in God grew, and he learned that God always keeps his promises. Abraham and Sarah were rewarded with abundance and a son.

GENESIS 18:10; 21:2

God Keeps His Promises

Sometimes friends will make promises that they cannot keep, and it will leave you sad and disappointed. You may even feel that there is no one that you can trust in this world. The good news is that God keeps his promises. When you don't know whom to trust, start with God. The path that he selects for you may not be the one that you envisioned, and your journey may be longer than expected. You may have moments of doubt and darkness, but in the midst of your darkness, there will always be a small beacon of light that leads you to your truth.

THREE WAYS TO GROW IN FAITH

1. Read your Bible daily. Identify 5 passages that you find inspiring, write them down and keep them close to your heart.

2. Read stories of everyday miracles. There are still miracles happening in the world today.

3. Write your biggest, wildest dream and believe that you can achieve it.

MY NOTES

MY NOTES

GROWING
IN
COURAGE

For God has not given us a spirit of
fear and timidity, but of power, love,
and self-discipline.

2 Timothy 1:7

OUR HERO

God called **DAVID** a man after God's own heart. As a boy, David was small in stature but courageous. He spent his time taking care of sheep and nurturing his relationship with God. David's father sent him to check on his brothers who were soldiers. David discovered that the giant and bully Goliath threatened his nation but all the soldiers were afraid of fighting him. One day, David, armed with a slingshot and his faith in God, stepped out of the shadows, did not give in to his fears, and bravely fought Goliath. David used a slingshot to defeat Goliath and saved his nation.

1 Samuel 17

You have a Brave Heart

Wouldn't it be great to be called a child after God's own heart? Well, you are. You were made in God's image. You may not look strong or feel brave, but courage will come right when you need it the most. Bravery is standing up to a bully; bravery is walking away from a fight, even when it may make your friends think that you are weak; and bravery is speaking a kind word when anger would be justified.

OUR HERO

DANIEL was an honorable man. He believed in God and prayed to him three times a day. Daniel was a friend of the king, and his friendship with the king made other men in the kingdom jealous. They tried but couldn't find fault with Daniel, so they convinced the king to pass a law that required everyone to pray to the king, even Daniel. Daniel refused to pray to the king because he only believed in praying to God. The king gave in to pressure from the men who were jealous of Daniel and reluctantly threw Daniel in a den with lions. Daniel continued to pray to God and the lions did not harm him. The king was happy that Daniel was not harmed.

DANIEL 6

Roar to Your Own Beat

Are you the child that wants to play chess when everyone else is playing sports? Maybe you are the only child in the cafeteria that is a vegetarian or the only one who kneels to pray before every game. You must always be willing to listen to the opinion of others with an open mind and heart; however, when your core beliefs are tested, do not be afraid to stand up for your beliefs. "No" is a short but powerful word that should be used generously in the face of temptation. The long and lonely walk away from the crowd is fraught with doubt when your greatest desire at the moment is to fit in. Remember that you were made to be unique, to stand out from the crowd, and to sometimes take the road only traveled by those with courage.

THREE WAYS TO GROW IN COURAGE

1. Whenever you feel fearful, remember that God is always with you.

2. Identify something or someone that causes you fear and write how you will overcome that fear.

3. Draw a picture of yourself as a biblical or modern-day superhero. What characteristics make you amazing?

MY NOTES

MY NOTES

GROWING IN LEADERSHIP

But it is not this way with you, but the
one who is the greatest among you must
become like the youngest, and the leader
like the servant.

Luke 22:26

OUR HERO

MOSES was chosen by God to bring the Israelites, who had been enslaved for over one hundred years, out of Egypt. The king of Egypt would not let the Israelites leave Egypt. As a leader, Moses had to keep the Israelites from losing faith, while God worked on their behalf. The King of Egypt was stubborn; he only obeyed God after God punished him with plagues, such as locusts, boils, hail, frogs and darkness over the earth. The journey to the land that God promised the Israelites was long, and the people grew weary and questioned Moses's leadership. Moses remained strong through many trials and led his people to the promised land. As a leader, Moses encouraged his people when they had doubts, gave them God's law (the 10 Commandments), asked God to forgive them when they sinned, and protected them from their enemies. Moses has been remembered through the generations for his strong leadership in the face of doubters and immeasurable obstacles.

EXODUS 3–16

Let Your Light Shine

We all crave love and acceptance. On the first day of a new school, church, or job, you just want to blend in with everyone else. You pray to God that nothing about you makes you seem different from the group. It is possible to spend a lifetime trying to walk, talk, dress, and act in a manner that will allow you to fit in with the crowd. Do not hide the unique gifts that God has bestowed on you by trying to be like everyone else. When you are called to lead, step out from the others and answer the call. Pray for the strength, wisdom, and patience to lead with confidence, to be faithful to your mission, and to inspire everyone around you.

OUR HERO

SOLOMON was a king who could ask God for anything. He wisely chose to ask God for a wise and understanding heart, so that he could judge his people fairly and rule with both strength and wisdom. Solomon's gift of wisdom was tested when two women claimed the same baby. Solomon threatened to harm the baby, knowing that the real mother would do anything to ensure the safety of her baby. As Solomon predicted, the baby's real mother offered to give the baby to the woman who was lying because the baby's safety was the most important thing to her. What a wise strategy by Solomon and a wise decision by the baby's mother!

1 KINGS 3

A Kind Heart + an Informed Mind = Wisdom

Should you study or play video games, play soccer or take piano lessons, tell your parents the truth or lie to avoid punishment? The wise decision is not always the easy decision. You are a unique being, so the right path for your friend may be the wrong path for you. Wisdom is when the thoughts in your head are in harmony with the feelings in your heart. A little uncertainty is normal, but your decisions should make you feel good and proud of yourself. A sinking feeling in the pit of your stomach is not a good indicator of a wise decision. Pray for wisdom, listen for guidance, and follow your heart. If you choose the wrong path, do not let pride or fear of embarrassment prevent you from changing course.

THREE WAYS TO GROW IN LEADERSHIP

1. Volunteer to serve in your church, school, or community.

2. Your opinions matter. Politely speak what is on your mind and in your heart, even if nobody else agrees with you.

3. The only way to make wise decisions is to practice. Think of a problem. For example, you witness a child being subjected to daily bullying. As a leader, your only choice is to take action. What steps can you take to help? Write ways of solving the problem. Explain the pros/cons of each, and support your final decision.

MY NOTES

MY NOTES

GROWING IN HAPPINESS

OUR HERO

God created **ADAM** and blessed him with a wonderful wife, EVE, and the
Garden of Eden. Adam and Eve had everything that they needed to be
very happy. They were surrounded by beautiful flowers and trees, they
had dominion over the animals and they had everything that they needed
to eat and drink. God only had one rule—do not eat from the Tree of Life.
Without a full appreciation of their blessings, Adam and Eve disobeyed
God. God exiled them from the Garden of Eden. Adam's eyes were opened,
and he realized that the devil had tricked him into believing that his life
was imperfect and he was missing something that he already had. Outside
of the Garden of Eden, Adam and Eve were responsible for their own food
and their own survival.

GENESIS 2-3

Showers of Blessings

You already have everything that you need to live a happy and successful life. Material things can enhance your daily life, but the happiness that you receive from material things is short lived. Real happiness comes from within your soul. Don't wait until you have lost something or someone that is important to you before you count your blessings. Carry the spirit of gratitude with you wherever you go.

JOSEPH'S brothers felt that their father, Jacob, loved Joseph more than them. His brothers became jealous and sold Joseph into slavery. Joseph had every reason to be unhappy. However, even as a slave, Joseph did not lose faith in God. He was a hard worker and was blessed with the ability to interpret dreams. Joseph focused on his blessings, not his problems. Joseph's ability to interpret dreams enabled him to warn the king of a famine. Joseph was no longer a slave; he was appointed to manage the stockpiling of food in preparation for the famine. When the famine came, his brothers were starving and went to Egypt to find food. Joseph's brothers were shocked to learn that Joseph was alive and that he was no longer a slave. After searching his soul, he forgave his brothers, saved them from starvation, and reunited his family. Joseph's act of forgiveness brought he and his family great joy.

GENESIS 37–45

Forgiveness Makes the Heart Happy

Forgiveness is freedom! You cannot always prevent someone from hurting you physically or emotionally, but God has given you the power to heal yourself. Imagine how you would feel if a good friend or a sibling did or said something inappropriate and you got punished for his or her actions. What if he or she did not acknowledge the wrong or defend you? The person that has hurt you can make amends, but they cannot heal you. Acknowledge that your feelings have been hurt and learn a lesson from the experience. Forgive, even when no one apologizes to you, and move beyond the pain. This is the most precious gift that you can give yourself.

THREE WAYS TO GROW IN HAPPINESS

1. Think about the last time that you were super happy? Remember that feeling. Keep a diary of happy moments or create a happiness jar.

2. Happiness is a choice. Practice choosing to be happy when you have a legitimate reason to be sad.

3. Tell someone that has hurt your feelings that you love and forgive him or her.

MY NOTES

MY NOTES

GROWING IN GRATITUDE

Colossians 4: 2

OUR HERO

Jesus told the beautiful story of a **GOOD SAMARITAN** who helped a stranger who fell among thieves. The thieves stole his clothes, wounded him, and left him almost dead. A priest saw the wounded man but passed him by on the other side of the street. Likewise, a Levite stopped to look at him but also passed him by. However, a Samaritan saw him and had compassion for him. The Samaritan poured oil on the injured man's wounds, bandaged them, placed the man on his donkey, and took him to an inn where he could receive care. When the Samaritan departed, he gave the host money to take care of the stranger.

LUKE 10:30-37

Give Abundantly

When you have a grateful heart, you can't help counting your blessings and then sharing them with others. Never shy away from sharing an idea, a kind word, a hug, a helping hand, or your worldly possessions with someone in need. We live in poverty—poverty of currency, love, and great ideas. The world is filled with people who are in need; however, the world is also filled with an abundance of wealth, more than enough for everyone to live a comfortable life. If we all counted our blessings and then shared them with our neighbors, near and far, all our lives would be richer. Ask God to deepen the love in your heart for your neighbors and to also enlarge your territory so that you have more to give. Then choose to be a giver and give abundantly!

OUR HERO

HANNAH did not have any children and this made her very sad. Other women teased her and made her feel like she was a failure. Hannah prayed to God and promised him that if he gave her a son, she would make sure that her son served God every day. God granted Hannah's wish, and she had a boy, named Samuel. Hannah thanked God and showed her gratitude by letting Eli, the priest, raise Samuel in the teachings of the Lord. Samuel grew up to be a great judge who was faithful to God. God abundantly blessed Hannah with several other children.

1 SAMUEL **1-2**

Recognize your Blessings and Give Thanks to God.

God has blessed you with a strong character, a kind heart, and the emotional and mental intelligence to use your talents for good. You have everything you need, but you may not realize it as yet and you may not have someone in your life to encourage and support you. If someone is teasing or bullying you, it is not your fault. That person does not realize that he or she is a child of God and has not grown into his or her own greatness, so he or she is unable to see how special you are. Be your own cheerleader and recognize that God is quietly cheering for you. Once you recognize that you are abundantly blessed, give God thanks and do something kind for someone else.

THREE WAYS TO GROW IN GRATITUDE

1. Say a prayer of thanksgiving when you awake and before bedtime.

2. Have a smile for everyone you meet and say thanks to everyone who helps you during the day.

3. Incorporate service into your daily life. What are twelve ways that you can be of service to your community?

MY NOTES

MY NOTES

GROWING IN CONFIDENCE

Have I not commanded you? Be strong and courageous! Do not tremble or be dismayed, for the LORD your God is with you wherever you go.

Joshua 1:9

OUR HERO

JOB was blessed with wealth and seven sons. He loved and trusted in God. Satan believed that Job was only being loyal to God because everything was going well in Job's life. But God believed in Job, so he allowed Satan to test him. Job lost all of his sons and wealth, and his body was ravaged with disease. Job suffered greatly and wondered what he had done wrong to lose all his blessings. Job realized that, sometimes, bad things happen to those who love God. Job persevered by constantly praying to God and having candid conversations with God. Job sought to understand why he was suffering. God restored Job's wealth, health, and family to him.

JOB 1–42

You Are Strong Enough to Pass Any Test

Nothing will ever happen to you that you and God cannot handle together. If the grade on your report card is an F, don't accept that it means "failure"; believe that it means "fearlessly working toward an A." Problems can shake you, but if you remain optimistic even in your weakest moments, they will not break you. When bad things happen, God is still with you and will not give you more challenges than you can handle. Take a mental picture of the best day or moment of your life; place that memory in your pocket and never leave home without it. Reflect on that memory when it seems as if everything is going wrong.

OUR HERO

RUTH, a Moabite, was married to NAOMI's son, an Israelite and they lived in Moab. Unfortunately, both women lost their husbands and Naomi decided to return home to Israel. It would have been easier for Ruth to remain in her homeland but Ruth loved Naomi very much and did not want her elderly mother-in-law to be alone. When Naomi urged her to stay in Moab, Ruth replied, "Don't ask me to leave you or to turn back from you. Where you go I will go, and where you stay, I will stay. Your people will be my people and your God my God." Ruth accompanied Naomi back to Israel. Ruth's loyalty was rewarded when she married Naomi's wealthy relative Boaz, who was able to financially support both Ruth and Naomi.

RUTH 1

You Are Never Alone

Imagine how great you would feel to hear a friend say, "I will love you always, and I will never leave you." Those powerful words resonate in the soul because we are all connected and we love when someone that we care about acknowledges that connection. Loyalty, love, and friendship are virtues that God has bestowed on us, and we are supposed to pass them on. Take a friend's hand, look into her eyes, and share a kind thought. If you are moved by Ruth and Naomi's story but feel that you have never experienced a deep friendship, you are wrong. God is with you now and has always been with you. There will be times when you will feel lonely but please know that you are never alone. You don't have to know how to pray to talk to God. Simply say, "Hi."

THREE WAYS TO GROW IN CONFIDENCE

1. Think of the last time that you cried or felt deep pain. You may have felt hopeless, like things would not get better, but they did. Meditate on that reality when you feel helpless.

2. What are three things that you know for sure (e.g., There is a God. My mother loves me. I am a great soccer player.)?

3 What is your biggest challenge? Write three possible solutions, pray for the right answer, and have confidence that God will always help you find the right solution.

MY NOTES

SONS AND DAUGHTERS,

GREATNESS = LOVE IN ACTION

I hope that you have enjoyed discovering all the unique things about yourself that makes you great and learning all the ways that you can continue growing into greatness. As you continue to define your own greatness, here are a few words from Jesus about greatness. Jesus stated, *"Whosoever will be great among you, let him be your minister. And whosoever will be chief among you, let him be your servant."* Matthew 20:20-28

Although some may define greatness as exercising dominion and authority over others, Jesus saw greatness as ministering to others and being of service. All God's children should aspire to be great! What a wonderful way to honor the legacy of Jesus! We are all made with unique gifts and talents. Our job is to recognize our uniqueness, discover the gifts that we are blessed with, develop and nurture those gifts, and then use them in service to our communities. If you were blessed with a wonderful voice, use it to inspire others. If you were blessed with a skill that leads to personal wealth, use your wealth to help the needy. If you have the talents to be a great leader, lead with compassion. If you were blessed with the gift of service, serve others with warmth and kindness. Strive for excellence in all that you do and be of good service to others. When you use your talents to be of service to others, you reach for the stars and get rewarded with showers of blessings.

After reading this book, I hope that you can confidently say the following:

I am a child of God!

God made me and molded me with only the finest ingredients.

Greatness is already within me; I embrace it.

God created a path for my life that is sometimes beautiful, sometimes challenging, but always filled with opportunities for me to learn and grow.

With God's help, I will grow into my greatness!

Thank you for reading this book! Enjoy every moment of the journey to becoming men and women after God's own heart. You are growing into greatness, and I am proud of you!

Janet Autherine

GROWING INTO GREATNESS WITH GOD

7 Paths to Greatness for Our Sons & Daughters

JOURNAL AND WORKBOOK

IT BEGINS WITH PRAYER

Prayer - Growing into Greatness with God

Dear God, thank you for making me in your own image. You are an awesome God, and I am grateful for all the blessings that you have bestowed on me. Please help me to have faith in you and rise above my doubts. Please help me to put my trust in you. When you call me to lead, please give me the strength and wisdom to do so in your honor. Please help me to be brave, especially when I look or feel weak. Please help me to have a spirit of understanding and forgiveness when I have been hurt. Please help me to love myself as much as you love me and to show love to you and my neighbors in thoughts, emotions, words, and deeds. When I am faced with challenges, please help me to remember that you are always with me so that I will stay strong, remain hopeful, and be faithful to your words. Thank you for walking with me and allowing me to grow into greatness with you.

QUESTIONS FOR STUDY AND SELF-REFLECTION

Reflect on the Seven Paths to Greatness. Our heroes have created their own path. List some fun ways that you can grow into greatness through Love, Faith, Courage, Leadership, Happiness, Gratitude, and Confidence. Share your ideas with your parents.

WRITE YOUR DEFINITION OF GREATNESS

Although we all love to receive praise,
your opinion of yourself is the only one
that truly matters.

What does greatness mean to you?

What steps can you take today to grow into greatness?

When I envision God, do I see a reflection of myself?

Do I realize that I am unique, or do I always want to fit in with the crowd?

Do I believe that God is my father, my best friend, and my biggest supporter?

Whom do I trust enough to turn to when I have to make tough decisions?

Do I find strength and courage in knowing that I am a child of God?

How has God blessed me? How have I expressed my gratitude?

What do I feel is missing from my life?

How has my faith been tested?

How do I react when I experience doubt?

_____

_____

_____

_____

_____

Are my mind and heart open to experience God's blessings, both seen and unseen?

_____

_____

_____

_____

_____

Do I take God with me to school, concerts, or sporting matches?

When was the last time that I stood up for myself, my beliefs, or my friend?

How have I helped someone in need?

_____

_____

_____

_____

_____

Do I believe in miracles?

_____

_____

_____

_____

_____

If I could ask God for one thing, what would it be?

Do I need to extend forgiveness to someone who has hurt me?

Do I need to forgive myself for something I did or said?

What is my definition of love?

Does the love in my heart shine through in my words and deeds?

How do I cope when something bad or unfair happens to me?

How do I react in the face of peer pressure?

Do I have a value or belief that I would not compromise?

What has been the best moment of my life, thus far?

_____

_____

_____

_____

_____

_____

_____

_____

_____

_____

MY NOTES

MY NOTES

MY NOTES

MY NOTES

About Janet Autherine

"Greatness is finding your natural talent, fueling it with passion, planting it in well-nourished soil, and toiling in the garden until it breaks through the earth and reaches for the stars."

Janet Autherine was born in St. Thomas, Jamaica, and immigrated to the United States when she was twelve. She grew up in Philadelphia and went on to study at Pennsylvania State University and Boston College Law School. After launching her law career in Washington, D.C., she was eventually drawn back to the sunshine, and she now lives in Florida with her three sons.

Autherine's faith in God has strengthened and sustained her through many challenges, and she is passionate about empowering children to love themselves and to grow into their greatness. Her juvenile nonfiction book Growing into Greatness with God is inspired by her own experience raising her sons to recognize and nourish what God has planted within each of them. You can also find her work at **www.JanetAutherine.com**.

Made in the USA
Columbia, SC
08 November 2018